Explore
the Continents

Explore
North America

Molly Aloian & Bobbie Kalman

🍄 Crabtree Publishing Company

www.crabtreebooks.com

A Bobbie Kalman Book

Dedicated by Katherine Berti
Mojej kochanej matce chrzestnej, Cioci Jadzi Sobolewskiej.

Editor-in-Chief
Bobbie Kalman

Writing team
Molly Aloian
Bobbie Kalman

Substantive editor
Kathryn Smithyman

Editors
Michael Hodge
Kelley MacAulay

Photo research
Crystal Sikkens

Design
Katherine Berti

Production coordinator
Heather Fitzpatrick

Prepress technician
Nancy Johnson Bosch

Consultant
Richard S. Hyslop, Professor of Geography,
Department of Geography & Anthropology,
California State Polytechnic University, Pomona

Illustrations
Barbara Bedell: pages 4 (bird and leaves), 6, 14 (sea otter), 18 (leaves),
    19, 23, 26
Samantha Crabtree: pages 7 (map), 24, 30, 31
Antoinette "Cookie" DeBiasi: page 5
Katherine Berti: pages 4 (map), 14 (fish), 15, 17, 22 (snake)
Robert MacGregor: front cover (map), back cover (map), pages 8-9, 12,
    14 (map), 16, 18 (map), 20 (map), 22 (map)
Margaret Amy Salter: pages 7 (butterflies), 20 (prairie dog)

Photographs
Dreamstime.com: Andrei Kaplun: page 12; Juan Lobo: page 29
iStockphoto.com: back cover, pages 10, 11 (bottom), 13, 21, 22, 23, 24,
    25, 28, 31
Travel Ink Photo Library/Index Stock: page 27
© Shutterstock: July Flower: page 15; Mike Norton: front cover;
    Sherry Yates Sowell: page 6
Other images by Corbis, Corel, Digital Stock, Digital Vision, and Photodisc

Library and Archives Canada Cataloguing in Publication

Aloian, Molly
    Explore North America / Molly Aloian & Bobbie Kalman.

(Explore the continents)
Includes index.
ISBN 978-0-7787-3075-0 (bound)
ISBN 978-0-7787-3089-7 (pbk.)

    1. North America--Geography--Juvenile literature.
I. Kalman, Bobbie, 1947- II. Title. III. Series.

E38.5.A46 2007   j917   C2007-900731-7

Library of Congress Cataloging-in-Publication Data

Aloian, Molly.
    Explore North America / Molly Aloian & Bobbie Kalman.
        p. cm. -- (Explore the continents)
    Includes index.
    ISBN-13: 978-0-7787-3075-0 (rlb)
    ISBN-10: 0-7787-3075-1 (rlb)
    ISBN-13: 978-0-7787-3089-7 (pb)
    ISBN-10: 0-7787-3089-1 (pb)
    1. North America--Juvenile literature. 2. North America--
Geography--Juvenile literature. I. Kalman, Bobbie. II. Title.
III. Series.

    E38.5.A45 2007
    970--dc22

                                                    2007003499

Crabtree Publishing Company

Printed in Canada/062017/TT20170515

www.crabtreebooks.com   1-800-387-7650

Published in Canada
Crabtree Publishing
616 Welland Ave.
St. Catharines, Ontario
L2M 5V6

Published in the United States
Crabtree Publishing
PMB 59051
350 Fifth Ave., 59th Floor
New York, NY 10118

Published in the United Kingdom
Crabtree Publishing
Maritime House
Basin Road North, Hove
BN41 1WR

Published in Australia
Crabtree Publishing
3 Charles Street
Coburg North
VIC, 3058

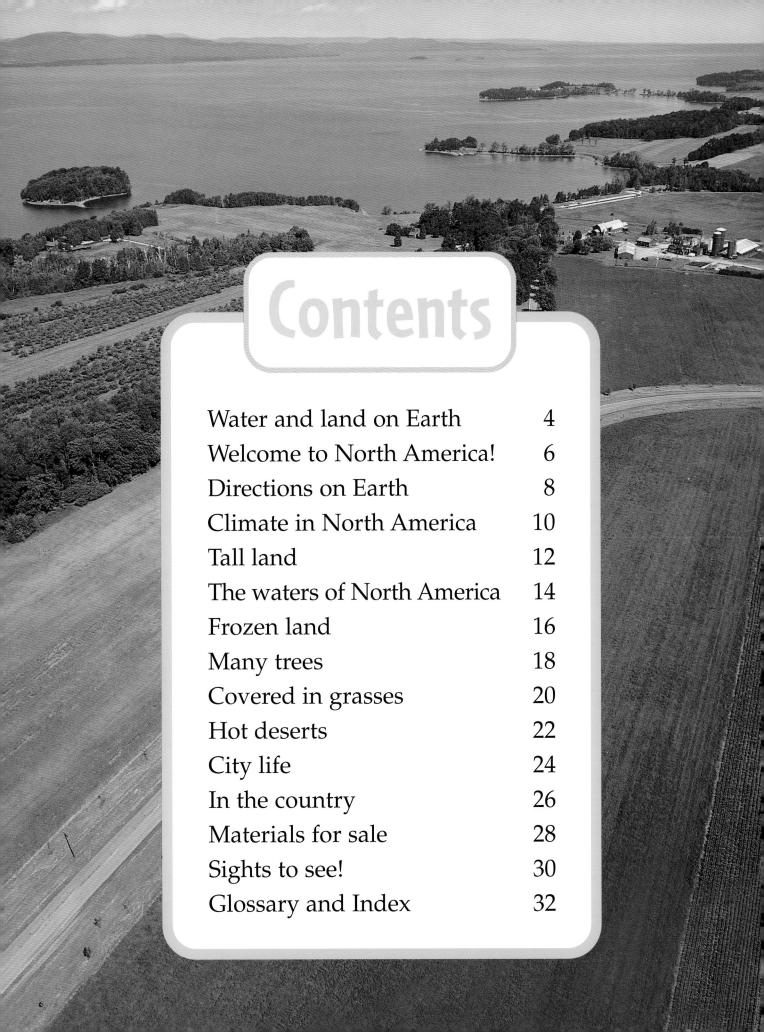

Contents

Water and land on Earth

There are large areas of water on Earth. These areas of water are called **oceans**. There are five oceans. From largest to smallest, they are the Pacific Ocean, the Atlantic Ocean, the Indian Ocean, the Southern Ocean, and the Arctic Ocean.

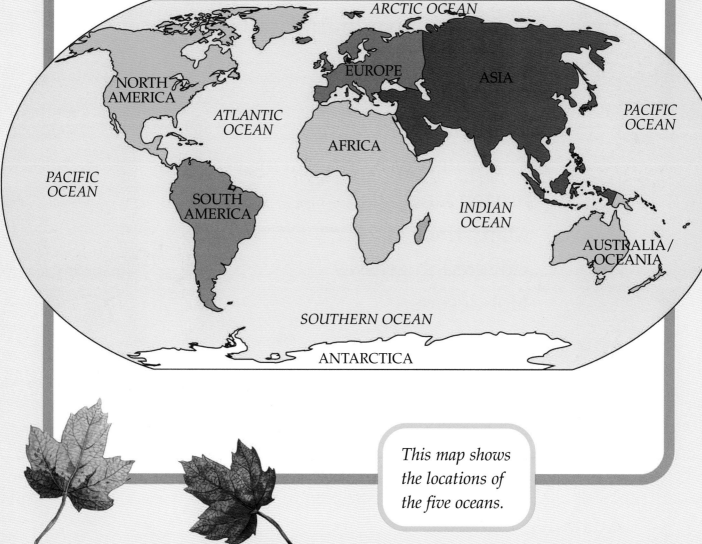

This map shows the locations of the five oceans.

*This bear lives in a **forest** in North America.*
To read more about forests, turn to page 18.

The continents

There are also seven gigantic areas of land on Earth. These areas of land are called **continents**. The continents are Asia, Africa, North America, South America, Antarctica, Europe, and Australia/Oceania.

Welcome to North America!

This book is about the continent of North America. There are 24 **countries** in North America. Each country has a boundary called a **border**. One country ends and another country begins at a border. A country also has a **government**. A government is a group of people who rule a country.

This picture shows colorful homes in a country called the Bahamas.

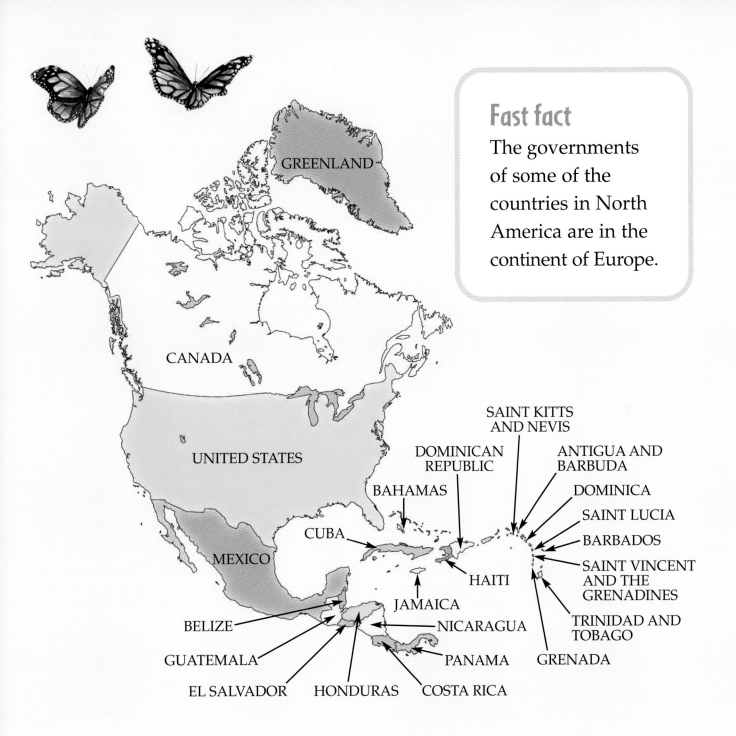

GREENLAND

CANADA

UNITED STATES

MEXICO

BAHAMAS

CUBA

HAITI

JAMAICA

DOMINICAN REPUBLIC

SAINT KITTS AND NEVIS

ANTIGUA AND BARBUDA

DOMINICA

SAINT LUCIA

BARBADOS

SAINT VINCENT AND THE GRENADINES

TRINIDAD AND TOBAGO

GRENADA

BELIZE

GUATEMALA

EL SALVADOR

HONDURAS

NICARAGUA

PANAMA

COSTA RICA

Island countries

Some countries are **islands**. An island is land that is surrounded by water. Islands are smaller than continents are. Some countries are made up of one island. Other countries are made up of many islands. The Bahamas, for example, is made up of about 700 islands!

Directions on Earth

There are four main **directions** on Earth. The four main directions are north, south, east, and west. The most northern place on Earth is the **North Pole**. The most southern place on Earth is the **South Pole**. In areas near the North Pole and the South Pole, the weather is always cold.

EQUATOR

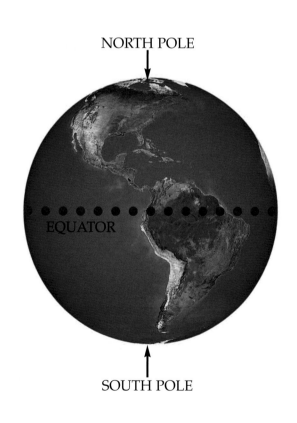

NORTH POLE

EQUATOR

SOUTH POLE

Hot near the equator

Areas near the **equator** are always hot. The equator is an imaginary line that separates Earth into two equal parts.

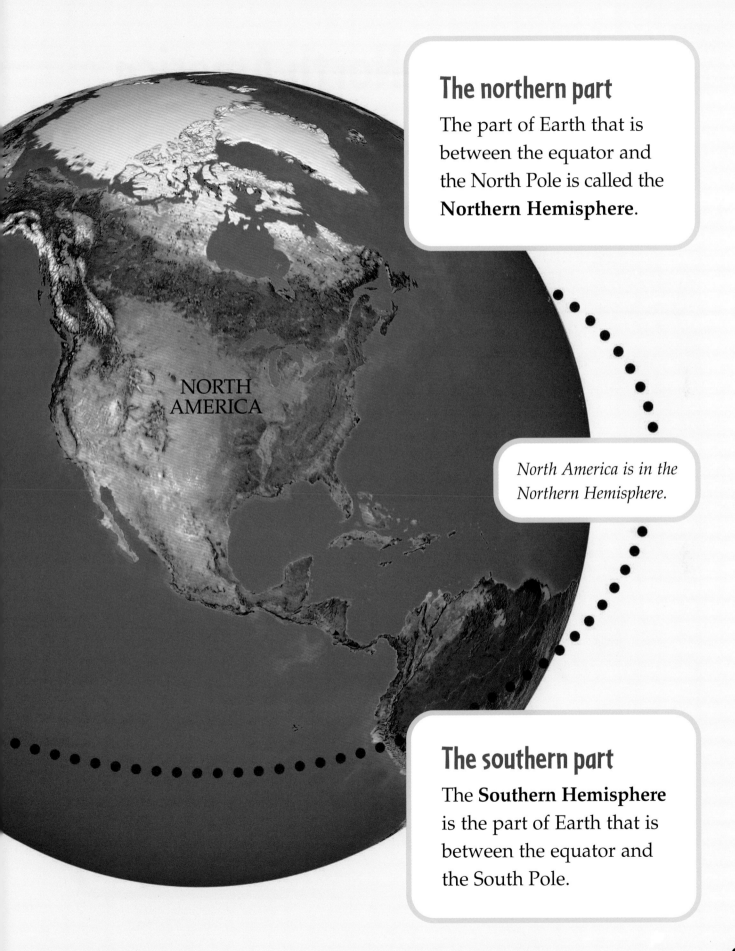

The northern part

The part of Earth that is between the equator and the North Pole is called the **Northern Hemisphere**.

North America is in the Northern Hemisphere.

NORTH AMERICA

The southern part

The **Southern Hemisphere** is the part of Earth that is between the equator and the South Pole.

Climate in North America

The Caribbean is close to the equator. The temperature in the Caribbean is warm all year long.

Climate is the weather that an area has had for a long period of time. Climate includes the temperature and the amount of rain and wind an area receives.

Cold or hot?

The northern parts of North America are far from the equator. In northern areas, the climate is cold, windy, and snowy all year long. The southern parts of North America are close to the equator. In most southern areas, the climate is hot and rainy year round.

Receiving rain

Some parts of North America receive a lot of rain or snow each year. Other parts of North America get almost no rain or snow each year.

This picture shows an area of the United States that receives very little rain.

The climate is cold, windy, and snowy in the northern parts of North America. These polar bears live in the northern part of North America.

Tall land

There are many **mountains** in North America. A mountain is a tall area of land. Mountains are a kind of **landform**. Landforms are different shapes on Earth's surface.

The brown areas on this map show where some of North America's mountains are.

mountains

All in a line

There are **mountain ranges** in North America. A mountain range is a group of mountains in a line. The Rocky Mountains form a mountain range in the western part of North America.

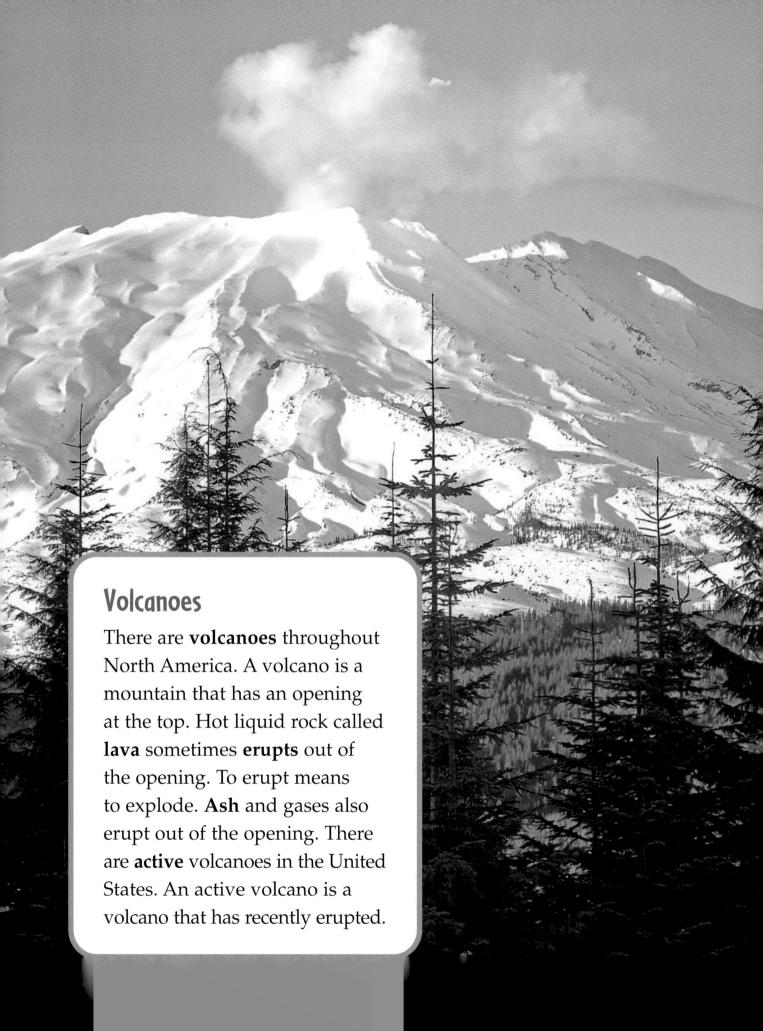

Volcanoes

There are **volcanoes** throughout North America. A volcano is a mountain that has an opening at the top. Hot liquid rock called **lava** sometimes **erupts** out of the opening. To erupt means to explode. **Ash** and gases also erupt out of the opening. There are **active** volcanoes in the United States. An active volcano is a volcano that has recently erupted.

The waters of North America

North America has oceans along all of its **coasts**. A coast is the area of land that is near an ocean. The northern coast of North America is near the Arctic Ocean. The eastern coast is near the Atlantic Ocean. The western coast is near the Pacific Ocean.

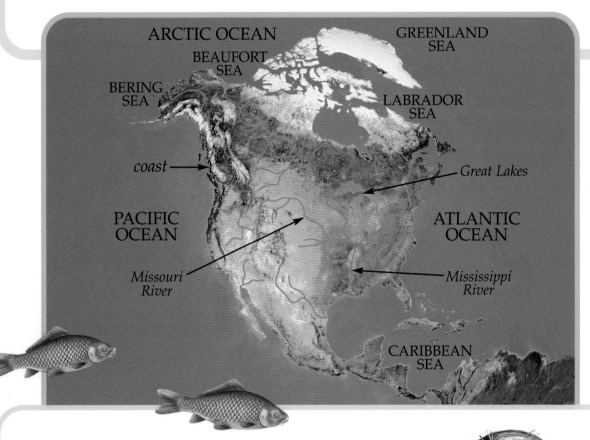

ARCTIC OCEAN

GREENLAND SEA

BEAUFORT SEA

BERING SEA

LABRADOR SEA

coast

Great Lakes

PACIFIC OCEAN

ATLANTIC OCEAN

Missouri River

Mississippi River

CARIBBEAN SEA

See the seas

There are also **seas** in North America. A sea is an area of an ocean that is partly surrounded by land.

Rippling rivers and large lakes

There are hundreds of **rivers** and **lakes** in North America. The Mississippi River and the Missouri River are two of the largest rivers in North America. In the eastern part of the continent, there is a group of five large lakes. These lakes are called the **Great Lakes**. The Great Lakes are Lake Huron, Lake Ontario, Lake Michigan, Lake Erie, and Lake Superior.

Fast fact

The first letter of each of the Great Lakes makes up the word "homes." Name the lakes without looking.

There are hundreds of other lakes in North America, but the Great Lakes are the largest lakes. This picture shows a lighthouse above Lake Superior.

THE GREAT LAKES

Lake Superior

Lake Huron

Lake Michigan

Lake Ontario

Lake Erie

Frozen land

In the northern part of North America, there is a large area of frozen land. The frozen land is called the **tundra**. There are no trees on the tundra. The weather is very cold and windy. Winter lasts almost the entire year! The weather becomes warm for only a few weeks in summer. Some small plants grow on the tundra during summer.

tundra

This arctic wolf lives on the cold tundra.

These arctic foxes have warm fur on their bodies.

Tundra animals

Animals such as musk oxen, arctic foxes, and snowy owls live on the tundra. Musk oxen and arctic foxes have thick layers of fur covering their bodies. Snowy owls have warm feathers. Fur and feathers keep these animals warm in the cold weather.

snowy owl

musk ox

Many trees

There are **forests** in North America. Forests are areas where many trees grow. **Coniferous trees** and **broadleaved trees** grow in North American forests. Coniferous trees have cones and needle-shaped leaves. Broadleaved trees have wide, flat leaves. In many forests, there are only coniferous trees. Some forests have only broadleaved trees. Other forests have both kinds of trees.

forests

What lives in forests?

Other plants, such as **ferns**, **mosses**, and shrubs, also grow in forests. Thousands of different animals live in North American forests! There are huge moose and tiny insects. Other forest animals include deer, wolves, porcupines, and rabbits.

Pine martens spend a lot of time in forests.

Covered in grasses

There are **grasslands** in the middle of North America. These grasslands are called **prairies**. Prairies are large areas of flat land. Many kinds of grasses grow there. Some shrubs and a few types of trees also grow on prairies. The prairies stretch from the southern part of Canada to the southern part of the United States.

grasslands

Many kinds of animals, such as this pronghorn, live on the prairies. Prairie dogs also live on prairies.

prairie dog

Fast fact

Plants called purple prairie clover grow on some prairies.

Tall, short, and mixed

There are three different types of prairies in North America. There are **tallgrass prairies**, **shortgrass prairies**, and **mixed-grass prairies**. In tallgrass prairies, grasses can grow to be over five feet (1.5 m) tall. In shortgrass prairies, grasses grow to be only about two feet (0.6 m) high. Both tall grasses and short grasses grow in mixed-grass prairies.

Hot deserts

There are **deserts** in North America. Deserts are very hot, dry areas. Deserts receive less than 10 inches (25 cm) of rain each year. The Sonoran Desert, the Mojave Desert, and the Chihuahuan Desert are three deserts in North America.

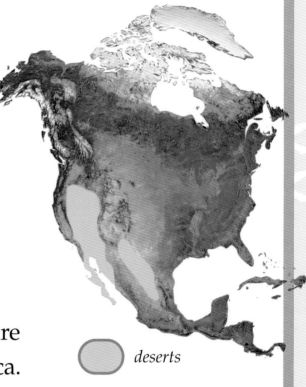

deserts

This hiker is standing in Death Valley. Death Valley is in the Mojave Desert. It is the hottest and driest part of North America.

The Sonoran Desert

The Sonoran Desert is in the southern part of the United States and in the northern part of Mexico. Plants such as the saguaro cactus, shown left, grow in the Sonoran Desert. Animals such as desert cottontail rabbits, desert tortoises, and horned lizards also live there. Over one million people live in the Sonoran Desert. The people live in cities and towns.

desert tortoise

desert cottontail rabbit

City life

Over 500 million people live in North America! Most people in North America live in **urban areas**. Urban areas are cities and towns. Toronto, Mexico City, and New York City are three large cities in North America. Over 5 million people live in Toronto. Over 18 million people live in Mexico City. Over 15 million people live in New York City.

This picture shows a **cathedral** in Mexico City.

The locations of some of the largest cities in North America are shown on this map.

This picture shows part of the city of Toronto. Toronto is in Canada. The tallest building in the picture is called the CN Tower. It is 1,815 feet (553 m) tall!

This picture shows part of New York City. This city is near the east coast of the United States.

In the country

Some people in North America live in **rural areas**. A rural area is a place in the countryside, outside a city or town. There are huge farms in rural areas of Canada and the United States. This picture shows cows that live on a large farm called a **ranch**. People **breed** and raise cows on the ranch. The cows are used for their milk and their meat.

These cows are being fed on a ranch.

*People buy and sell fruit and vegetables at **markets**. This market is in Guatemala.*

Rural Central America

The southernmost part of North America is often called **Central America**. Central America is made up of Guatemala, Belize, Honduras, El Salvador, Nicaragua, Costa Rica, and Panama. There are many rural areas in Central America. Some of the people who live in these areas work on coffee, sugar cane, or banana **plantations**. There are very few schools or businesses in rural areas, so many people have no jobs. Without jobs, it is hard for people to feed their families or find good places to live.

Materials for sale

People in North America sell materials that are found in nature. They sell the materials to make money. The materials that people sell include oil, **timber**, wheat, and corn. Timber is wood that is cut and prepared so people can use it to build things. Oil and timber are found in the United States, Canada, and Central America. Wheat and corn grow mainly in the United States and Canada.

This truck is carrying a huge load of wood that will be used as timber.

Metal materials

Nickel, copper, silver, and gold are other natural materials found in North America. They are types of metals. People dig these metals out of **mines**. A mine is a large hole that is dug into the ground. People use the metals to make many things, such as jewelry and coins.

This picture shows a large mining truck at a copper mine.

Sights to see!

There are many beautiful places to see and interesting things to do in North America. These pages show a few of North America's spectacular sights!

Mayan pyramids

The Mayans were highly **civilized** people who lived in Mexico, Guatemala, Belize, and El Salvador thousands of years ago. They built **pyramids** in the places where they lived. The pyramids still stand today! People from all over the world travel to see these pyramids.

Niagara Falls

Niagara Falls is a very exciting place to visit. Niagara Falls is a gigantic waterfall on the Niagara River. Thousands of people visit Niagara Falls each year. The falls can be seen from both Canada and the United States.

Hawaii

Hawaii is far from the rest of North America. It is in the middle of the Pacific Ocean! Hawaii is part of the United States, however. Many people visit Hawaii to see beautiful animals such as whales, dolphins, and sea turtles.

Glossary

Note: Boldfaced words that are defined in the text may not appear in the glossary.

ash A powdery gray substance that shoots out of volcanoes

breed To cause animals of the same species to mate and have babies

cathedral A very large church

civilized Describing people with an advanced society and way of life

fern A plant with big leaves and no flowers

lake A large area of water surrounded by land

market A place where people sell fruits, vegetables, and other items

moss Small green plants that grow in groups on rocks or on trees

plantation A large farm on which crops are grown

pyramid A large structure with a square or triangular bottom and sloping sides that meet in a point at the top

ranch A large farm on which one type of animal is raised

river A large area of water that flows into an ocean, a lake, or another river

the Caribbean An area made up of the Caribbean Sea, its coasts, and the islands in the Caribbean Sea

Index